EMMANUEL JOSEPH

The Business of Balance, Politics, Psychology, and Health in a Connected World

Copyright © 2025 by Emmanuel Joseph

All rights reserved. No part of this publication may be reproduced, stored or transmitted in any form or by any means, electronic, mechanical, photocopying, recording, scanning, or otherwise without written permission from the publisher. It is illegal to copy this book, post it to a website, or distribute it by any other means without permission.

First edition

This book was professionally typeset on Reedsy.
Find out more at reedsy.com

Contents

1	Chapter 1: Introduction to Balance	1
2	Chapter 2: The Role of Politics in Shaping Balance	3
3	Chapter 3: Psychological Dimensions of Balance	5
4	Chapter 4: Health as a Pillar of Balance	7
5	Chapter 5: The Intersection of Politics and Psychology	9
6	Chapter 6: Health Policies and Political Balance	11
7	Chapter 7: Psychological Resilience in a Connected World	13
8	Chapter 8: The Impact of Technology on Balance	15
9	Chapter 9: Social Media and Mental Health	17
10	Chapter 10: The Role of Education in Promoting Balance	19
11	Chapter 11: Balancing Work and Life in a Digital Age	21
12	Chapter 12: The Global Perspective on Balance	23
13	Chapter 13: The Role of Media in Shaping Perceptions of...	25
14	Chapter 14: Environmental Sustainability and Balance	28
15	Chapter 15: The Future of Balance in a Connected World	30
16	Chapter 16: Strategies for Achieving Balance	32
17	Chapter 17: Conclusion and Call to Action	34

1

Chapter 1: Introduction to Balance

In today's interconnected world, achieving balance has become an increasingly elusive goal. Whether it's in politics, psychology, or health, the intricate webs that link various aspects of our lives call for a nuanced understanding of how these domains interact. The pursuit of balance is not merely a personal endeavor but a societal one, requiring concerted efforts from individuals, communities, and institutions alike. This introductory chapter sets the stage for exploring the multifaceted nature of balance, highlighting its significance in an era marked by rapid technological advancements and global interconnectedness.

The concept of balance extends beyond the individual, encompassing broader societal structures. In the realm of politics, balance is essential for fostering stability and ensuring that the needs of diverse populations are met. Political systems that embrace inclusivity and equitable governance are better equipped to navigate the complexities of modern society. Similarly, psychological balance is vital for personal well-being and collective mental health. In a world where digital communication and social media dominate, maintaining psychological equilibrium has become increasingly challenging, yet critically important.

Health, as a foundational pillar of balance, cannot be overlooked. The interconnectedness of physical, mental, and societal health underscores the importance of a holistic approach to well-being. Public health policies and access to healthcare services play a crucial role in promoting balance within communities. The global nature of health challenges, such as pandemics, further emphasizes the need for collaborative efforts and resilient healthcare systems.

In this chapter, we will explore the overarching themes of balance that will be further elaborated in the subsequent chapters. By understanding the interplay between politics, psychology, and health, we can begin to grasp the complexities of achieving balance in a connected world. The journey towards balance is ongoing, and it is only through collective efforts and a holistic approach that we can hope to achieve a harmonious and equitable society.

2

Chapter 2: The Role of Politics in Shaping Balance

Politics, as the driving force behind societal governance, plays a critical role in shaping the conditions for balance. Policies and decisions made at the political level have far-reaching implications for economic stability, social justice, and public health. In this chapter, we delve into the intricate relationship between politics and balance, examining how political ideologies, power dynamics, and governance structures influence the equilibrium within societies. We also explore the challenges and opportunities presented by democratic and autocratic systems in fostering balance.

Political ideologies often serve as the foundation for governance structures and policy decisions. These ideologies, whether rooted in conservatism, liberalism, socialism, or other schools of thought, shape the priorities and approaches of political leaders. The balance within a society is heavily influenced by how these ideologies are implemented, as they dictate the distribution of resources, the protection of rights, and the establishment of social norms. This section will explore how different political ideologies impact the quest for balance, with examples from various countries and historical contexts.

Power dynamics within political systems also play a crucial role in shaping balance. The concentration of power in the hands of a few can lead to imbalances in societal structures, often resulting in inequality and social unrest. Conversely, a more equitable distribution of power can foster a sense of inclusivity and fairness, promoting stability and harmony. This section will analyze the impact of power dynamics on balance, with case studies illustrating the consequences of both centralized and decentralized power structures.

Governance structures, whether democratic, autocratic, or hybrid, influence the ability of societies to achieve balance. Democratic systems, with their emphasis on participation and representation, offer opportunities for diverse voices to be heard and considered in decision-making processes. Autocratic systems, while often more efficient in decision-making, may struggle to maintain balance due to limited avenues for dissent and accountability. This section will explore the strengths and weaknesses of different governance structures in promoting balance, highlighting examples from around the world.

In conclusion, the role of politics in shaping balance cannot be overstated. Political ideologies, power dynamics, and governance structures all contribute to the conditions necessary for achieving equilibrium within societies. By understanding these factors, we can better appreciate the complexities of balance in the political realm and work towards more inclusive and equitable governance.

3

Chapter 3: Psychological Dimensions of Balance

The human psyche is a complex and dynamic entity, constantly seeking equilibrium. Psychological balance, often referred to as mental well-being, is essential for individuals to thrive in a connected world. This chapter explores the various psychological factors that contribute to balance, including stress management, emotional regulation, and cognitive resilience. We also examine the impact of social media and digital communication on mental health, highlighting the need for strategies to maintain psychological balance in an increasingly digital landscape.

Stress management is a key component of psychological balance. In our fast-paced, connected world, individuals are often subjected to high levels of stress, which can negatively impact mental and physical health. Effective stress management techniques, such as mindfulness, exercise, and time management, are essential for maintaining balance. This section will explore various stress management strategies and their effectiveness in promoting psychological well-being.

Emotional regulation, the ability to manage and respond to emotions in a healthy way, is another crucial aspect of psychological balance. Emotions can influence our thoughts, behaviors, and interactions with others, making emotional regulation vital for maintaining harmony within ourselves and our relationships. This section will delve into the importance of emotional intelligence, strategies for emotional regulation, and the impact of unregulated emotions on psychological balance.

Cognitive resilience, the ability to adapt and bounce back from adversity, is essential for navigating the complexities of modern life. In a world where change is constant, cognitive resilience enables individuals to maintain balance and thrive despite challenges. This section will explore the concept of cognitive resilience, factors that contribute to its development, and practical strategies for building resilience in everyday life.

The impact of social media and digital communication on mental health is a growing concern in our connected world. While these technologies offer opportunities for connection and information sharing, they can also contribute to stress, anxiety, and feelings of inadequacy. This section will examine the psychological effects of social media, strategies for maintaining a healthy digital presence, and the importance of digital detoxes in promoting psychological balance.

In conclusion, achieving psychological balance requires a multifaceted approach that addresses stress management, emotional regulation, cognitive resilience, and the impact of digital communication. By understanding and implementing strategies to promote psychological well-being, individuals can navigate the complexities of modern life and maintain equilibrium in a connected world.

4

Chapter 4: Health as a Pillar of Balance

Health is a fundamental pillar of balance, serving as the foundation upon which all other aspects of life are built. This chapter delves into the interconnections between physical health, mental well-being, and societal stability. We explore the role of preventive healthcare, access to medical services, and public health policies in promoting balance. Additionally, we discuss the impact of global health crises, such as pandemics, on the equilibrium of societies and the importance of resilience in the face of such challenges.

Preventive healthcare is a crucial component of maintaining balance. By focusing on prevention rather than treatment, individuals and societies can reduce the burden of disease and promote overall well-being. This section will explore the importance of preventive measures, such as vaccinations, regular health check-ups, and healthy lifestyle choices, in maintaining physical and mental health.

Access to medical services is another vital factor in promoting balance within societies. Equitable access to healthcare ensures that all individuals, regardless of socioeconomic status, can receive the care they need to maintain their health. This section will examine the challenges and opportunities in providing accessible healthcare, with examples from different countries and healthcare systems.

Public health policies play a significant role in shaping the health of populations and promoting balance. Effective policies can address health disparities, improve access to care, and promote healthy behaviors. This section will explore the impact of public health policies on societal well-being, with case studies highlighting successful initiatives and areas for improvement.

Global health crises, such as pandemics, have a profound impact on the balance of societies. These crises test the resilience of healthcare systems, economies, and communities, often revealing existing vulnerabilities. This section will discuss the lessons learned from past pandemics, the importance of preparedness and resilience, and strategies for maintaining balance in the face of global health challenges.

In conclusion, health is a cornerstone of balance, encompassing preventive care, access to medical services, and effective public health policies. By addressing these areas and fostering resilience, individuals and societies can achieve and maintain equilibrium in the face of health challenges.

5

Chapter 5: The Intersection of Politics and Psychology

The intersection of politics and psychology is a critical area of study in understanding balance. Political decisions and policies can significantly influence psychological well-being, while public sentiment and mental health can, in turn, shape political landscapes. This chapter examines the bidirectional relationship between politics and psychology, highlighting case studies that illustrate the impact of political events on collective mental health. We also discuss the role of psychological insights in informing political strategies and fostering balanced governance.

Political decisions often have profound effects on the mental health of populations. Policies related to economic stability, social welfare, and healthcare access can either alleviate or exacerbate psychological stress. For example, economic recessions and austerity measures can lead to increased anxiety, depression, and social unrest, whereas policies that support job security, mental health services, and social safety nets can promote psychological well-being. This section will explore these dynamics, with real-world examples illustrating the psychological impact of political decisions.

Public sentiment and collective mental health can also influence political landscapes. High levels of public stress, fear, or anger can lead to political movements, changes in voter behavior, and shifts in policy priorities. For instance, the collective anxiety and uncertainty during economic crises or health pandemics can fuel populist movements and demand for policy changes. This section will examine how public mental health shapes political outcomes, drawing on historical and contemporary examples.

Psychological insights can inform political strategies and contribute to balanced governance. Understanding the psychological needs and motivations of populations can help political leaders craft policies that promote well-being and stability. For example, incorporating principles of fairness, transparency, and inclusivity can foster trust and cooperation among citizens. This section will discuss the application of psychological theories in political decision-making and highlight successful case studies where such approaches have led to balanced outcomes.

In conclusion, the interplay between politics and psychology is a vital aspect of achieving balance within societies. Political decisions impact psychological well-being, while public mental health can shape political landscapes. By recognizing and addressing these interconnections, political leaders can foster balanced and resilient societies.

6

Chapter 6: Health Policies and Political Balance

Health policies are a crucial component of achieving balance within societies. This chapter explores the role of government initiatives and policies in promoting public health and ensuring equitable access to healthcare services. We examine the challenges faced by policymakers in addressing health disparities and the impact of political ideologies on health policy decisions. Additionally, we discuss the importance of international cooperation and collaboration in addressing global health issues and achieving a balanced approach to public health.

Government health policies play a significant role in shaping the overall health of populations. Policies that promote preventive care, access to medical services, and health education can lead to improved health outcomes and reduced healthcare costs. This section will explore various health policy initiatives, such as universal healthcare systems, vaccination programs, and public health campaigns, highlighting their impact on population health and societal balance.

Addressing health disparities is a critical challenge for policymakers. Social determinants of health, such as income, education, and living conditions, can lead to significant health inequities within and between populations. This section will examine strategies for reducing health disparities, such as targeted interventions, community health programs, and policies aimed at improving the social determinants of health. Case studies will illustrate successful approaches to addressing health inequities and promoting balance.

Political ideologies significantly influence health policy decisions. Ideological beliefs about the role of government, individual responsibility, and social justice shape the priorities and approaches of political leaders. For example, conservative ideologies may prioritize personal responsibility and market-based solutions, while progressive ideologies may emphasize government intervention and universal access to healthcare. This section will explore how different political ideologies impact health policy and the pursuit of balance.

International cooperation and collaboration are essential for addressing global health issues and achieving a balanced approach to public health. Health challenges, such as pandemics, climate change, and antimicrobial resistance, transcend national borders and require coordinated efforts. This section will discuss the importance of international partnerships, global health organizations, and cross-border initiatives in promoting global health and balance. Case studies of successful international collaborations will highlight the potential for collective action in addressing global health challenges.

In conclusion, health policies play a crucial role in promoting balance within societies. Government initiatives, efforts to address health disparities, the influence of political ideologies, and international cooperation all contribute to the overall health and well-being of populations. By implementing balanced and equitable health policies, societies can achieve better health outcomes and greater stability.

7

Chapter 7: Psychological Resilience in a Connected World

In an interconnected world, psychological resilience is more important than ever. This chapter delves into the concept of resilience, exploring its psychological underpinnings and the factors that contribute to its development. We discuss the role of individual and collective resilience in navigating the complexities of modern life and maintaining balance. Case studies and personal narratives illustrate the diverse ways in which people build and sustain resilience in the face of adversity.

Resilience is the ability to adapt and thrive in the face of challenges, adversity, and change. It is a dynamic process that involves a combination of psychological, emotional, and behavioral factors. This section will explore the psychological foundations of resilience, including self-efficacy, optimism, and emotional regulation. By understanding these underlying factors, individuals can develop strategies to enhance their resilience and maintain balance in their lives.

Individual resilience is shaped by personal experiences, coping mechanisms, and social support networks. This section will examine the various factors that contribute to individual resilience, such as a strong sense of purpose, healthy relationships, and effective stress management techniques. Personal narratives and case studies will provide insights into how individuals from diverse backgrounds have navigated challenges and built resilience.

Collective resilience, on the other hand, refers to the ability of communities and societies to withstand and recover from adverse events. This section will explore the importance of social cohesion, community support, and shared values in fostering collective resilience. Examples of communities that have demonstrated remarkable resilience in the face of natural disasters, economic crises, and social upheaval will be highlighted to illustrate the power of collective action.

The digital age presents unique challenges to psychological resilience. While technology offers opportunities for connection and information sharing, it can also contribute to stress, anxiety, and social isolation. This section will discuss strategies for maintaining resilience in the digital age, such as setting boundaries, practicing mindfulness, and fostering meaningful offline connections. By balancing digital and real-world interactions, individuals can enhance their resilience and thrive in a connected world.

In conclusion, psychological resilience is a crucial factor in achieving balance in a connected world. By understanding the psychological underpinnings of resilience and implementing strategies to enhance individual and collective resilience, individuals and communities can navigate the complexities of modern life and maintain equilibrium.

8

Chapter 8: The Impact of Technology on Balance

Technology has revolutionized the way we live, work, and interact, but it also presents unique challenges to achieving balance. This chapter examines the dual-edged nature of technology, exploring its benefits and drawbacks in the context of politics, psychology, and health. We discuss the impact of digital communication on mental well-being, the role of technology in shaping political landscapes, and the implications of technological advancements for public health. Strategies for harnessing technology to promote balance are also explored.

Digital communication has transformed the way we connect with others, providing unprecedented opportunities for social interaction and information sharing. However, it can also contribute to stress, anxiety, and social isolation. This section will explore the psychological impact of digital communication, highlighting the importance of setting boundaries, practicing mindfulness, and maintaining face-to-face connections to promote mental well-being in a digital age.

Technology plays a significant role in shaping political landscapes, influencing how information is disseminated, political campaigns are conducted, and public opinions are formed. Social media platforms, in particular, have become powerful tools for political engagement and mobilization. This section will examine the impact of technology on politics, discussing both the positive and negative implications of digital political engagement, as well as strategies for fostering informed and balanced political participation.

In the realm of public health, technological advancements have led to significant improvements in medical care, disease prevention, and health monitoring. Innovations such as telemedicine, wearable health devices, and data-driven healthcare have the potential to enhance health outcomes and promote balance. However, these advancements also raise ethical and privacy concerns. This section will explore the implications of technology for public health, discussing both the benefits and challenges of integrating technology into healthcare systems.

In conclusion, technology has a profound impact on various aspects of balance in our lives. By understanding its benefits and drawbacks, we can develop strategies to harness technology in ways that promote mental well-being, informed political engagement, and improved health outcomes. Achieving balance in a connected world requires mindful and intentional use of technology, ensuring that it serves as a tool for enhancing our lives rather than a source of imbalance.

9

Chapter 9: Social Media and Mental Health

Social media has become an integral part of modern life, influencing how we communicate, perceive ourselves, and interact with the world. This chapter explores the complex relationship between social media and mental health, highlighting the potential benefits and risks associated with its use. We examine the impact of social media on self-esteem, anxiety, and depression, as well as the role of online communities in providing support and fostering resilience. Strategies for maintaining a healthy balance in social media usage are also discussed.

The impact of social media on self-esteem is a significant concern in the digital age. The constant exposure to curated and idealized representations of others' lives can lead to feelings of inadequacy and low self-worth. This section will explore the psychological effects of social comparison on social media, discussing strategies for mitigating its negative impact and promoting a healthy sense of self-esteem.

Anxiety and depression are also linked to excessive social media use. The pressure to present a perfect online persona, fear of missing out (FOMO), and cyberbullying can contribute to heightened anxiety and depressive symptoms. This section will examine the ways in which social media can exacerbate these mental health issues and provide practical tips for managing social media use to reduce anxiety and depression.

Despite these challenges, social media also offers opportunities for connection and support. Online communities can provide a sense of belonging, emotional support, and access to resources for individuals struggling with mental health issues. This section will highlight the positive aspects of social media, showcasing examples of online support groups, mental health campaigns, and digital platforms that promote well-being and resilience.

In conclusion, social media has both positive and negative implications for mental health. By adopting mindful and intentional practices, individuals can maintain a healthy balance in their social media use, leveraging its benefits while mitigating its risks. Strategies such as setting boundaries, curating a positive online environment, and seeking support from online communities can help promote mental well-being in a connected world.

10

Chapter 10: The Role of Education in Promoting Balance

Education plays a vital role in fostering balance within individuals and societies. This chapter explores the importance of educational systems in promoting psychological well-being, civic engagement, and public health. We discuss the impact of curriculum design, teaching methodologies, and educational policies on achieving balance. Additionally, we examine the role of lifelong learning and continuous personal development in maintaining equilibrium in an ever-changing world.

Curriculum design is a fundamental aspect of promoting balance through education. A well-rounded curriculum that includes subjects such as social-emotional learning, critical thinking, and health education can equip students with the skills and knowledge needed to navigate the complexities of modern life. This section will explore the impact of comprehensive and inclusive curricula on students' mental well-being, civic engagement, and overall development.

Teaching methodologies also play a crucial role in fostering balance. Educators who adopt student-centered, inclusive, and adaptive teaching approaches can create supportive and engaging learning environments. This section will discuss various teaching methodologies that promote psychological well-being, resilience, and a love for learning. Case studies of successful educational practices will illustrate the positive impact of these approaches.

Educational policies at the national and institutional levels influence the overall effectiveness of educational systems in promoting balance. Policies that prioritize equitable access to education, support for diverse learning needs, and mental health resources can create conditions for balanced development. This section will examine the role of educational policies in fostering balance, with examples of successful policy initiatives from around the world.

Lifelong learning and continuous personal development are essential for maintaining balance in an ever-changing world. The rapid pace of technological advancements and societal changes necessitates ongoing learning and adaptation. This section will explore the importance of lifelong learning, discussing strategies for fostering a growth mindset, self-directed learning, and continuous personal development.

In conclusion, education is a powerful tool for promoting balance within individuals and societies. By designing comprehensive curricula, adopting inclusive teaching methodologies, implementing supportive educational policies, and fostering a culture of lifelong learning, we can equip individuals with the skills and knowledge needed to achieve and maintain balance in a connected world.

11

Chapter 11: Balancing Work and Life in a Digital Age

The digital age has blurred the boundaries between work and personal life, making it increasingly challenging to achieve balance. This chapter delves into the complexities of work-life balance, exploring the impact of remote work, digital communication, and technological advancements on personal well-being. We discuss strategies for setting boundaries, managing stress, and fostering a healthy work-life balance in a connected world. Case studies and personal stories provide insights into the diverse ways individuals navigate this challenge.

Remote work, while offering flexibility and convenience, can also lead to a blurring of the lines between work and personal life. The lack of physical separation between the workplace and home can result in longer working hours, increased stress, and difficulties in disconnecting from work. This section will explore the benefits and challenges of remote work, discussing strategies for creating a structured work environment, setting clear boundaries, and maintaining a healthy work-life balance.

Digital communication tools have transformed the way we collaborate and interact in the workplace. While these tools facilitate real-time communication and collaboration, they can also contribute to information overload and constant connectivity. This section will examine the impact of digital communication on work-life balance, offering practical tips for managing digital distractions, prioritizing tasks, and ensuring meaningful offline interactions.

Technological advancements have also introduced new complexities in achieving work-life balance. The proliferation of smartphones, email, and instant messaging means that employees are often expected to be available around the clock. This section will discuss the importance of setting boundaries with technology, such as implementing digital detoxes, establishing designated work hours, and practicing mindfulness to maintain a healthy balance.

In conclusion, achieving work-life balance in the digital age requires intentionality and proactive strategies. By setting boundaries, managing stress, and fostering healthy work habits, individuals can navigate the complexities of modern work environments and maintain equilibrium in their personal and professional lives.

12

Chapter 12: The Global Perspective on Balance

Achieving balance is not solely an individual or national endeavor; it requires a global perspective. This chapter explores the interconnectedness of the world and the importance of international cooperation in promoting balance. We examine the role of global institutions, cross-cultural exchanges, and international policies in fostering equilibrium. Case studies of successful global initiatives highlight the potential for collective action in addressing global challenges and achieving balance.

The interconnectedness of the world means that issues such as climate change, economic inequality, and public health crises transcend national borders. This section will explore the importance of international cooperation in addressing these global challenges and promoting balance. We will discuss the role of global institutions, such as the United Nations, World Health Organization, and International Monetary Fund, in fostering collaboration and collective action.

Cross-cultural exchanges are essential for promoting understanding and empathy among diverse populations. Cultural diversity can enrich societies, foster innovation, and contribute to balanced perspectives. This section will examine the benefits of cross-cultural interactions, highlighting examples of successful cultural exchange programs, international collaborations, and global initiatives that promote mutual respect and understanding.

International policies play a crucial role in shaping global balance. Policies related to trade, environmental protection, human rights, and public health impact the stability and well-being of nations. This section will discuss the importance of equitable and inclusive international policies, with examples of successful policy initiatives that have contributed to global balance.

In conclusion, achieving balance requires a global perspective and collective action. By fostering international cooperation, cross-cultural exchanges, and equitable policies, we can address global challenges and promote balance on a global scale. The interconnectedness of our world calls for a collaborative approach to achieving equilibrium and fostering a harmonious and sustainable future.

13

Chapter 13: The Role of Media in Shaping Perceptions of Balance

Media plays a significant role in shaping public perceptions of balance. This chapter explores the influence of traditional and digital media on political opinions, mental health, and public health awareness. We examine the impact of media coverage on public sentiment, the role of media in promoting balance, and the challenges of navigating misinformation and bias. Strategies for media literacy and critical consumption of information are also discussed.

The media landscape has evolved dramatically in recent years, with the rise of digital platforms and social media transforming how information is disseminated and consumed. This section will explore the impact of traditional and digital media on political opinions, highlighting how media coverage can shape public perceptions and influence political outcomes. We will discuss the role of media in promoting transparency, accountability, and informed political engagement.

Media coverage also significantly impacts mental health. Sensationalist reporting, negative news cycles, and social media echo chambers can contribute to stress, anxiety, and a skewed perception of reality. This section will examine the psychological effects of media consumption, discussing strategies for maintaining mental well-being in a media-saturated environment. We will highlight the importance of balanced reporting and the role of media in promoting positive mental health.

Public health awareness is another area where media plays a crucial role. Media coverage of health issues, such as pandemics, vaccination campaigns, and public health initiatives, can influence public behavior and attitudes towards health. This section will explore the impact of media on public health awareness, discussing the importance of accurate and responsible reporting in promoting health literacy and positive health behaviors.

Case Study: Media's Role in the COVID-19 Pandemic

The COVID-19 pandemic provides a compelling case study of the media's role in shaping public perceptions of balance. Throughout the pandemic, media coverage played a crucial role in informing the public about the virus, government responses, and health guidelines. However, the media also faced challenges, including the spread of misinformation, sensationalist reporting, and public skepticism.

During the initial stages of the pandemic, accurate and timely media coverage was essential in raising awareness about the virus and promoting preventive measures. News outlets provided updates on case numbers, government policies, and health recommendations, helping the public stay informed and take necessary precautions.

However, the pandemic also saw the proliferation of misinformation and conspiracy theories, particularly on social media platforms. False claims about the virus, treatments, and vaccines spread rapidly, contributing to public confusion and mistrust. Media organizations had to navigate the challenge of debunking misinformation while providing reliable information to the public.

The case study of media's role in the COVID-19 pandemic highlights the importance of responsible reporting, media literacy, and critical consumption of information. By promoting accurate information and combating misinformation, the media can play a vital role in fostering balance and resilience in society.

In conclusion, media plays a significant role in shaping public perceptions of balance. By promoting transparency, accountability, and accurate information, the media can contribute to informed political engagement, positive mental health, and public health awareness. Developing media literacy and critical consumption skills are essential for navigating the complexities of the media landscape and maintaining balance in a connected world.

14

Chapter 14: Environmental Sustainability and Balance

The health of our planet is intrinsically linked to the balance of societies. This chapter explores the relationship between environmental sustainability and balance, highlighting the importance of sustainable practices in achieving equilibrium. We discuss the impact of environmental policies, climate change, and resource management on political stability, psychological well-being, and public health. Case studies of successful sustainability initiatives illustrate the potential for achieving balance through environmental stewardship.

Environmental sustainability is essential for maintaining balance within societies. Sustainable practices, such as renewable energy, conservation, and waste reduction, can mitigate the impact of human activities on the planet and promote long-term stability. This section will explore the importance of sustainable practices in achieving balance, discussing the role of governments, businesses, and individuals in promoting environmental stewardship.

Climate change is one of the most pressing global challenges, with far-reaching implications for political stability, public health, and psychological well-being. This section will examine the impact of climate change on balance, highlighting the importance of mitigation and adaptation strategies. We will discuss the role of international agreements, such as the Paris Agreement, in

CHAPTER 14: ENVIRONMENTAL SUSTAINABILITY AND BALANCE

fostering global cooperation and addressing climate change.

Resource management is another critical aspect of environmental sustainability. The sustainable use of natural resources, such as water, forests, and minerals, is essential for maintaining ecological balance and supporting human well-being. This section will explore strategies for sustainable resource management, including conservation efforts, responsible consumption, and innovative technologies.

Case Study: Denmark's Transition to Renewable Energy

Denmark provides a compelling case study of successful sustainability initiatives. The country has made significant strides in transitioning to renewable energy, with a strong focus on wind power. Denmark's commitment to renewable energy has not only reduced its carbon footprint but also promoted economic growth and energy security.

The Danish government's supportive policies and investment in renewable energy infrastructure have played a crucial role in the country's success. Initiatives such as feed-in tariffs, subsidies, and public-private partnerships have incentivized the development of wind farms and other renewable energy projects.

Denmark's transition to renewable energy serves as a model for other countries seeking to achieve environmental sustainability and balance. By prioritizing sustainable practices, investing in renewable energy, and fostering international cooperation, societies can promote environmental stewardship and achieve long-term equilibrium.

In conclusion, environmental sustainability is essential for achieving balance within societies. Sustainable practices, climate change mitigation, and responsible resource management are critical for promoting long-term stability and well-being. By learning from successful sustainability initiatives and fostering a culture of environmental stewardship, we can work towards a harmonious and balanced future.

15

Chapter 15: The Future of Balance in a Connected World

As we look to the future, achieving balance will remain a critical goal. This chapter explores emerging trends and potential challenges in the pursuit of balance in politics, psychology, and health. We discuss the role of innovation, technological advancements, and global cooperation in shaping the future of balance. Additionally, we examine the importance of adaptive strategies and resilience in navigating an ever-evolving world.

Emerging trends such as artificial intelligence, biotechnology, and renewable energy have the potential to transform various aspects of life, presenting both opportunities and challenges for achieving balance. This section will explore these trends, discussing their potential impact on political systems, mental well-being, and public health. We will also examine the ethical considerations and societal implications of these advancements.

Technological advancements, while offering numerous benefits, also pose new challenges for maintaining balance. The rapid pace of innovation can lead to disruptions in traditional industries, job displacement, and increased inequality. This section will discuss strategies for addressing these challenges, such as investing in education and workforce development, promoting inclusive policies, and fostering a culture of innovation and adaptability.

Global cooperation will continue to play a vital role in addressing the

CHAPTER 15: THE FUTURE OF BALANCE IN A CONNECTED WORLD

complex challenges of the future. Issues such as climate change, pandemics, and economic instability require coordinated efforts and collective action. This section will explore the importance of international collaboration, highlighting examples of successful global initiatives and the role of global institutions in promoting balance.

Adaptive strategies and resilience will be essential for navigating the uncertainties of the future. The ability to adapt to changing circumstances, recover from setbacks, and embrace new opportunities will be critical for maintaining balance. This section will discuss the importance of fostering a growth mindset, building psychological resilience, and developing adaptive policies and practices.

In conclusion, the future of balance in a connected world will be shaped by emerging trends, technological advancements, and global cooperation. By embracing innovation, fostering resilience, and promoting inclusive and adaptive strategies, we can navigate the complexities of the future and achieve a harmonious and balanced world.

16

Chapter 16: Strategies for Achieving Balance

In this penultimate chapter, we present practical strategies for achieving balance in various aspects of life. We discuss the importance of self-awareness, goal setting, and continuous personal development in maintaining equilibrium. Strategies for managing stress, fostering resilience, and promoting well-being in a connected world are explored. Case studies and personal anecdotes provide insights into the diverse ways individuals and communities strive for balance.

Self-awareness is a fundamental aspect of achieving balance. Understanding one's strengths, weaknesses, and personal needs can help individuals make informed decisions and set realistic goals. This section will explore techniques for developing self-awareness, such as mindfulness practices, self-reflection, and seeking feedback from others. By cultivating self-awareness, individuals can navigate life's challenges with greater clarity and confidence.

Goal setting is another crucial strategy for maintaining balance. Setting clear, achievable goals provides direction and motivation, helping individuals stay focused and organized. This section will discuss the principles of effective goal setting, including the SMART (Specific, Measurable, Achievable, Relevant, Time-bound) criteria. We will also explore the importance of flexibility and adaptability in adjusting goals as circumstances change.

CHAPTER 16: STRATEGIES FOR ACHIEVING BALANCE

Continuous personal development is essential for achieving and maintaining balance in an ever-evolving world. Lifelong learning, skill development, and personal growth contribute to a sense of fulfillment and resilience. This section will discuss strategies for continuous personal development, such as pursuing new interests, seeking opportunities for professional growth, and fostering a growth mindset.

Managing stress is a critical component of achieving balance. Chronic stress can undermine physical and mental well-being, making it important to develop effective stress management techniques. This section will explore various strategies for managing stress, including mindfulness practices, physical exercise, time management, and relaxation techniques. Personal anecdotes and case studies will illustrate the effectiveness of these approaches in promoting well-being.

Fostering resilience is another key strategy for maintaining balance. Resilience enables individuals to adapt to adversity, recover from setbacks, and thrive in the face of challenges. This section will discuss the importance of building resilience through positive relationships, self-care practices, and adaptive coping strategies. Examples of resilient individuals and communities will provide inspiration and practical insights.

In conclusion, achieving balance requires a multifaceted approach that includes self-awareness, goal setting, continuous personal development, stress management, and resilience. By implementing these strategies, individuals and communities can navigate the complexities of modern life and maintain equilibrium in a connected world.

17

Chapter 17: Conclusion and Call to Action

In the final chapter, we reflect on the themes explored throughout the book and the importance of balance in an interconnected world. We emphasize the need for collective action, empathy, and resilience in achieving and maintaining equilibrium. A call to action encourages readers to take proactive steps towards fostering balance in their own lives and communities. The journey towards balance is ongoing, and it is only through concerted efforts that we can hope to achieve a harmonious and connected world.

Throughout this book, we have examined the intricate interplay between politics, psychology, and health in the quest for balance. We have explored how political decisions shape societal conditions, how psychological resilience enables individuals to navigate challenges, and how health serves as a foundational pillar of well-being. We have also delved into the impact of technology, media, education, and environmental sustainability on achieving balance.

As we conclude this journey, it is essential to recognize that balance is not a static state but a dynamic process. It requires continuous effort, adaptation, and a commitment to personal and collective growth. The interconnectedness of our world means that the actions of individuals, communities, and nations

CHAPTER 17: CONCLUSION AND CALL TO ACTION

are intertwined, and achieving balance necessitates a collaborative approach.

Empathy is a crucial element in fostering balance. By understanding and appreciating diverse perspectives, we can build inclusive and compassionate societies. Empathy enables us to bridge divides, foster cooperation, and address the root causes of imbalances. This section will highlight the importance of empathy in achieving balance and provide practical tips for cultivating empathetic attitudes and behaviors.

Resilience is another vital component in maintaining balance. The ability to adapt to change, recover from setbacks, and embrace new opportunities is essential for navigating the uncertainties of the future. This section will discuss strategies for building resilience at both individual and collective levels, emphasizing the importance of supportive relationships, self-care practices, and adaptive mindsets.

The call to action encourages readers to take proactive steps towards fostering balance in their own lives and communities. This section will provide practical suggestions for achieving balance, such as engaging in civic activities, advocating for equitable policies, practicing mindfulness, and promoting sustainable practices. By taking small, meaningful actions, individuals can contribute to a broader movement towards a balanced and harmonious world.

In conclusion, the pursuit of balance is a shared responsibility that requires collective action, empathy, and resilience. By embracing these principles and taking proactive steps, we can navigate the complexities of modern life and work towards a more connected and balanced world. The journey towards balance is ongoing, and it is only through concerted efforts that we can hope to achieve a harmonious and equitable society.

The Business of Balance: Politics, Psychology, and Health in a Connected World

In our hyper-connected and fast-paced world, achieving a sense of balance can seem like an elusive goal. "The Business of Balance" dives deep into the intricate interplay between politics, psychology, and health, revealing how these domains shape and are shaped by each other in our quest for equilibrium.

Throughout the book, we explore the role of political ideologies and power dynamics in shaping societal conditions, the psychological underpinnings of resilience and well-being, and the fundamental importance of health as a cornerstone of balance. With the rise of digital communication and technological advancements, maintaining balance has become more complex, yet more crucial than ever.

Featuring compelling case studies and personal narratives, this book offers practical strategies for achieving balance in various aspects of life. From managing stress and building resilience to fostering informed political engagement and promoting sustainable practices, "The Business of Balance" provides a comprehensive roadmap for navigating the complexities of modern life.

By emphasizing the need for collective action, empathy, and resilience, this book calls on readers to take proactive steps towards fostering balance in their own lives and communities. "The Business of Balance" is not just a guide but a call to action, urging us all to contribute to a harmonious and connected world.

www.ingramcontent.com/pod-product-compliance
Lightning Source LLC
LaVergne TN
LVHW020457080526
838202LV00057B/5998